Clinging to Jesus

Clinging to Jesus

Praying & Meditating on God's Word When You're in Pain

Heather Hart

Clinging to Jesus
Praying & Meditating on God's Word When You're in Pain

2021 © Heather Hart
Edited by Valerie Riese
Cover design by Heather Hart
Cover photo © Leo Lintang | Deposit Photos

All rights reserved. No part of this publication may be reproduced, stored in a retrieval system, or transmitted by any means—electronic, mechanical, photographic (photocopying), recording, or otherwise—without prior permission in writing from the author, unless it is for the furtherance of the gospel, printed, and given away free of charge.

All scripture quotations, unless otherwise indicated, are taken from The Holy Bible, English Standard Version. ESV® Text Edition: 2016. Copyright © 2001 by Crossway Bibles, a publishing ministry of Good News Publishers.

Printed in the United States of America
ISBN: 9798723124417

Dedication

To my prayer partner, Sue Duff…
Thank you for always being there for me. For caring about more than my migraines. And reminding me that life isn't all about me.

To Beverly Kinnibrugh…
You are a dear friend, my health advocate, and so much more. I don't know where I would be without you, but life is much more fun with you in it. Even when my head hurts.

To Valerie Riese and the Candid Gals…
Your patience, understanding, encouragement, assistance, and prayers over the past several years have meant more to me than you will ever know. Thank you for being real.

To Pamela A. Taylor…
The best client anyone could ask for and a dear friend.
KLU GIB.

To my husband, Paul, and our five fantastic teens…
It's been a rough few years, but your love has never faltered. When I couldn't get out of bed, you came to me. When I needed quiet, you did your best. When I missed important events or couldn't pick you up from school, you never complained. You are the best family anyone could hope for and I am so blessed by you.

To Jesus…
None of this would be possible without You.

Contents

When It Hurts 9
Speak It 13
Pray It 19
Write It 25
Know It.. 29
See It 33
Hear It 37
Befriend It.. 41
Spill It 45
Play It 49
Embrace It... 53
About Heather Hart.. 57
Recommended Resources 61
Notes 63

When It Hurts

Do not be conformed to this world, but be transformed by the renewal of your mind…
Romans 12:2

In 2019, the CDC put together a National Health Interview Survey, and they found that over 20% of adults suffered from chronic pain[i]. In women alone it was almost 22%. That means one out of every five people have experienced chronic pain.

But chronic pain isn't the only kind of pain. Whether you have had a headache, back pain, sunburn, toothache, or kidney stones, you know how distracting pain can be. When you're in pain, it's hard to focus. Reading, praying, thinking; anything that requires brainpower is difficult to say the least.

The longer the pain lasts, the more our faith can suffer. If reading is hard, that means reading our Bibles becomes a challenge. Sitting down to pray can feel hopeless when pain consumes our thoughts. And that's what pain does: *it consumes us*. Or it can feel that way.

I know all this firsthand. I've had a migraine virtually every day for the past three and a half years. Not weeks, not months, *years*. There are days the only thought I can process is, "My head hurts."

It's easy to let the pain consume me—to dwell on the hurt. However, in the book of Romans, Paul wrote, "Do not be conformed to this world, but be transformed by the renewal of your mind."[ii] That's a reminder I need regularly. Instead of letting my pain consume me—instead of letting it conform me—I need to renew my mind in Jesus.

I can't say that I get it right 100% of the time, because I don't. There are days when I've cried out because I'm just sick of the pain. I'm sick of the way it has changed my life. And that's something that's important to know: pain does change your life. *Clinging to Jesus* isn't about how to overcome pain and regain the life you had before. That's an unrealistic expectation. *Clinging to Jesus* is about how to cling to Jesus when you're in pain.

The pain might not go away. We might have to learn to adapt—to change our definition of "normal." However, in the midst of our pain, we can still keep our eyes on

Christ. He can renew our faith every morning and help us get through the pain.

Even when we can't go to church. Even when we miss the fellowship of other believers. Even when we start to feel hopeless. God is always good. No matter how much pain we are in, we can fix our eyes on Jesus.

I don't know whether you are consumed by chronic pain, get a headache every now and then, have arthritis, or a sprained ankle, but I encourage you to stick with me through the pages of this book. I'm going to share ten easy ways to renew your mind in Christ. Ways to refocus on what God's Word says about your situation. Ways to take your pain to God in prayer.

Speak It

> How then will they call on him in whom they have not believed? And how are they to believe in him of whom they have never heard? And how are they to hear without someone preaching?
> Romans 10:14

I was terrified of stormy weather.

For as long as I can remember, when clouds rolled in and the air changed, my heart would start pounding. I never understood how others could calmly keep on doing whatever it was they were doing. I didn't grasp how they could act normal when a storm could start any moment.

Storms—as far as I could tell, they were dangerous and unpredictable.

One day, I was sitting outside reading the book of Job when I stumbled on something that forever changed the way I felt about storms. Paul wrote to Timothy that "All Scripture is breathed out by God and profitable for teaching…for training in righteousness, that the man of God may be complete."[iii] If you've ever wondered how Job's friends fit into that, this is it.

Elihu said of God:

> He draws up the drops of water, they distill his mist in rain, which the skies pour down and drop on mankind abundantly. Can anyone understand the spreading of the clouds, the thunderings of his pavilion? Behold, he scatters his lightning about him and covers the roots of the sea. For by these he judges peoples; he gives food in abundance. He covers his hands with the lightning and commands it to strike the mark. Its crashing declares his presence; the cattle also declare that he rises.
>
> Job 36:27-33

Elihu continues through Job 37, describing how great God is. But what really got me was how in control He is. God tells the rain to fall (v. 6). He breathes the ice and causes the lightning to shine (v. 15). His voice is the thunder we hear rumbling through the clouds (vv. 2, 4-5).

I remember thinking, *if God is in control of the storm, what is there for me to fear?*

When a storm blew in, I would pick up my Bible and read through Job 36 and 37. The words would calm my racing heart. But not just that: when my young children were frightened by the weather, I would read it to them. I remember telling them that God was in control.

Years later, when I was in the midst of my battle with chronic pain, it occurred to me that I needed to find a "Job 36" for when my head hurt. I needed to find a Scripture I could turn to when the pain was so great it was consuming me. It was at that time, God directed me to Psalm 69.

> Save me, O God! For the waters have come up to my neck. I sink in deep mire, where there is no foothold; I have come into deep waters, and the flood sweeps over me. I am weary with my crying out; my throat is parched. My eyes grow dim with waiting for my God.
>
> Deliver me from sinking in the mire; let me be delivered from my enemies and from the deep waters. Let not the flood sweep over me, or the deep swallow me up, or the pit close its mouth over me. Answer me, O Lord, for your steadfast love is good; according to your abundant mercy, turn to me. Hide not your face from your servant, for I am in distress; make haste to answer me. Draw near to my soul, redeem me; ransom me...
>
> But I am afflicted and in pain; let your salvation,

O God, set me on high! I will praise the name of God with a song; I will magnify him with thanksgiving. This will please the Lord more than an ox or a bull with horns and hoofs. When the humble see it they will be glad; you who seek God, let your hearts revive. For the Lord hears the needy and does not despise his own people who are prisoners. Let heaven and earth praise him, the seas and everything that moves in them. For God will save Zion and build up the cities of Judah, and people shall dwell there and possess it; the offspring of his servants shall inherit it, and those who love his name shall dwell in it.

Psalm 69: 1-3, 14-18, 29-36

Reading those verses aloud lets the words wash over my soul. When I read it in my head, the pain can be distracting and cause me to lose my place or not really comprehend what I'm reading. But when I read it aloud, it helps me focus.

I've also started reading Psalm 23 and Romans 8 aloud. Or anything I need to read but can't seem to focus on. However, one of my favorite things to read aloud is the poetic version of "The Gospel Narrative" from Milton Vincent's *Gospel Primer*. I had enjoyed reading it aloud even before my chronic pain journey began. The ebb and flow of the words have always spoken to my soul, and I lean into it even more so when my head hurts. It's during those moments when the pain is bad, I know I need Jesus to get me through.

Live It

Make a list of Scriptures or other writings you can read aloud when you're in pain and want to cling to Jesus. That way, when you hurt, you don't have to figure out how to refocus on Jesus, but you have an easy go-to guide.

Add your own favorites to the list below:

- Psalm 69
- Romans 8
- Psalm 23
- _____
- _____
- _____

Pray It

> This is the confidence that we have toward him,
> that if we ask anything according
> to his will he hears us.
> 1 John 5:14

Praying when you are in pain can seem impossible. Oftentimes the only prayer I can get out is "God, help," "Lord, make it stop hurting," "Help me endure," or even just, "Jesus, please." I simply don't have the brainpower for anything more. And God has shown me that's okay.

Our prayers don't have to be intricate. If all we can do is lie in bed and mutter a word or two towards Heaven, God still hears us. He is the God who hears: *El Shama*.[iv]

There is no more powerful example of this than in Matthew 14 when Peter walked on water. As he was walking on the stormy seas, Peter got overwhelmed by the wind and waves. So much so that he started to sink. But then he cried out, "Lord, save me!"

Immediately, Jesus reached out His hand, steadying him. And that's what He does for us when we cry out in our agony. Just as Jesus didn't stop the storm that scared Peter, He doesn't always take away the source of our pain. Instead, He will reach out and hold us close. He can calm our souls and help us refocus our minds, even as the pain remains.

In Matthew 11, Jesus said, "Come to me, all who labor and are heavy laden, and I will give you rest. Take my yoke upon you, and learn from me, for I am gentle and lowly in heart, and you will find rest for your souls."[v] Jesus is always with us,[vi] and never out of reach. Moreover, He knows what it is to be in pain.[vii] He hung on the cross in agony. He was whipped and beaten. I cannot even fathom the pain He endured because of His love for us.

And He willingly walked into that pain. In the garden of Gethsemane, He was so overcome by what lie ahead for Him, His sweat became like blood. The agony of the pain He would endure caused Him great distress, but He still walked into that pain for us. That's why we can pray with Him, "God, please take away the pain. Yet not as I will, but Your will be done."[viii]

We can remember the words of Jesus and pray, "I know in this world I will have trouble, help me keep my focus on You, the one who overcame the world."[ix] And pray with David, "When the pain is too much, Lord, Your steadfast love is enough for me. Give me strength and help me cling to You."[x]

We can also pray longer Scriptures. Years ago, I was introduced to the idea of using the Psalms as a blueprint for our prayers. Flipping through the Book of Psalms, you read through until one speaks to you (or systematically work your way through the entire book), and then turn it into a prayer.

Here's an example from Psalm 4 (starting with verse one):

1. "Answer me when I call, O God of my righteousness! You have given me relief when I was in distress. Be gracious to me and hear my prayer!"

> *Father God, I know You hear me. I am in so much pain right now. Please give me relief. Make the pain go away. In Your great mercy and grace, hear this plea, Lord.*

2. "O men, how long shall my honor be turned into shame? How long will you love vain words and seek after lies? Selah"

> *How long will this pain last? How long will it seem like my prayers go unanswered? Lord, let others see Your great mercy through the work You do in me. Don't let them use my pain as a way to speak lies about You.*

3. "But know that the Lord has set apart the godly for himself; the Lord hears when I call to him."

> *I know You hear me. I know I belong to You, even when*

it hurts.

4. "Be angry, and do not sin; ponder in your own hearts on your beds, and be silent. Selah"

> *Father, sometimes the pain is too much for me to bear. Help me to keep my eyes fixed on You. Don't let my pain hurt my faith in You. Remind me of Your faithfulness.*

5. "Offer right sacrifices, and put your trust in the Lord."

> *Lord, I trust in You. Even when I am in pain, I know You are good.*

6. "There are many who say, 'Who will show us some good? Lift up the light of your face upon us, O Lord!'"

> *God, You are good. Let the light of Your face shine upon me. Help me to see the blessings that are all around me.*

7. "You have put more joy in my heart than they have when their grain and wine abound."

> *Be the joy of my heart God. Whether I am in pain, or pain-free, let me live for You and You alone.*

8. "In peace I will both lie down and sleep; for you alone, O Lord, make me dwell in safety."

> *God, I know You are good. I trust that You can use all things for good, including this. Help me to remember how much You love me. In the name of Your Son, Jesus, I pray. Amen.*

This next thing might seem sort of silly. However, I've actually made up a little song to pray when I'm in pain. The familiar melody of "Rain, Rain, Go Away" makes this catchy prayer song easy for me to remember, and it also cheers up my heart. Probably because it is a little silly.

All that said, here's what I sing/pray some days:

> *Pain, pain, go away*
> *Take the hurt and help me pray*
> *Thank You Jesus for today.*

You can make up your own song, build on this, or have a good laugh at my expense. Whatever which way, I encourage you to find what works for you when you're in pain. Just don't let your pain keep you from Jesus.

Live It

What are some things you can pray when it hurts in addition to your own short prayers? Add to the list below so you have a quick reference:

- Psalm 61:1-3
- Psalm 130:1-6
- Psalm 69:1-3, 13-18
- Mark 9:24
- 1 Chronicles 4:10
- Jonah 2:2, 7, 9
- Psalm 94:18-19
- _____
- _____
- _____

Write It

> In the day of my trouble I call upon you,
> for you answer me.
> Psalm 86:7

I have never been one for prayer journaling. I know it's a wonderful spiritual practice, and I have many friends who fill entire journals with their prayers to God. It's just not… me. Which is probably ironic since I love to write.

I do, however, have a free-written prayer journal. I love the lack of structure freewriting offers. And writing out my prayers helps me to focus.

Here's how my prayer journal works:

On days I want to write or pray, and the words just won't come, I open a document on my computer and start typing out a prayer. I don't worry about using proper sentences, punctuation, or sounding pretty. It's just a conversation with Jesus about what's on my mind.

My prayer might be about what I need or want to be doing, and how my pain is keeping me from focusing. And eventually, my prayer may morph into what I should have been writing to start with. I might outline a blog post through prayer writing, or it could be about what we're going to have for supper. It's just a way to talk it out with Jesus.

The best part of this practice is that it helps me focus as it's totally informal. If I get distracted, I can quickly scan to see what I've already written or even just start a new paragraph with, "Well, I don't know where I was going with that, but…" and start an entirely different train of thought.

When my prayer time ends, I can look at all the words I've written, and I know my pain hasn't kept me from being with Jesus. Instead of walking away frustrated that I can't remember what I prayed about, it's all written out as a reminder that I took it all to God in prayer.

I save all my prayer entries in a folder on my computer, though I don't think I've ever gone back and re-read them.

You can, of course, handwrite prayers in this fashion as well. I have carpal tunnel, so to save myself additional pain it's better for me to type. Plus, I can type much faster than I can write freehand, thus my fingers keep up better when I'm on my computer.

Live It

I encourage you to try this method when you're not getting any prayer time no matter how much you try, or when you walk away from prayer frustrated that you can't remember what you prayed about. Would it be easier for you to handwrite in a journal or type entries on your computer?

Know It

> I shall not die, but I shall live,
> and recount the deeds of the Lord.
> Psalm 118:17

First Thessalonians 5:24 says, "The one who calls you is faithful, and he will do it."[xi] I learned that truth years ago. Whenever I feel like something is beyond me, I remember that if God called me to do it, He will make it come to pass. God called me to be a mom. To love my children. To point women to Jesus. If I believe He has called me to those things, I can know He will empower me to do them, even when I'm in pain.

I was still in my first year of migraines when I begged

the hospital staff to let me go because my family needed me. Then I got home and my head hurt so bad I couldn't get out of bed. I was useless. Sure, they loved me and were happy to see me, but my family didn't *need* me (and it's a good thing they didn't).

I remember lying in bed ready to give up. I was trying to think of graceful exit strategies for everything God had called me to. *God had called me to…* those words stopped me in my tracks. If God called me to do all those things, who was I to throw in the towel? If He called me to do it, I could trust He would give me the strength to carry on. When I can't get out of bed, when my house doesn't get cleaned, when I feel "less than," I can cling to the reminder that there is no condemnation for those who belong to Jesus.[xii]

I call these my "mustard seeds of faith." They are Bible promises I can cling to. They're facts I know to be true, facts I believe without a shadow of a doubt. Knowing what the Bible says keeps my faith on solid ground, even when my world seems to be spiraling out of control.

I've adapted a few Scriptures to cling to when dealing with chronic pain:

> God is always with me; even when I'm in pain. I can be confident that I am not alone in my struggle. (Based on Deuteronomy 31:8)
>
> God loved me so much, He sent His only Son to die for my sins. (John 3:16)
>
> And God's love for me will never fail. (Isaiah 54:10)

In my weakness, God is strong. (2 Corinthians 12:9-10; Isaiah 40:29)

In this world I will have trouble, but Jesus overcame the world. (John 16:33)

Even when I stumble, God has me in His hand. (Psalm 37:23-24)

God can use my pain for good. (Romans 8:28)

I don't have to be afraid, because God is with me. (Isaiah 43:2; Joshua 1:9)

I don't know what tomorrow will bring, but I know God will take care of me. (Matthew 6:25-34)

No matter how bad it hurts, no matter what I can't do, there is no condemnation for me because I belong to Jesus. (Romans 8:1)

But here's the thing: I know those things to be true, yet I don't always remember the book, chapter, and verse to go with them. Sometimes I just remember the Bible says something about boasting in my weakness. Or I might remember that God is always with me and take that opportunity to look up related Scriptures.

We don't have to memorize Scriptures word for word to know they are true. I once tried to memorize the entire book of Galatians... while I had a migraine. It didn't go so well. God wasn't asking me to do that. Knowing the entire book wouldn't help me when I needed to Cling to Jesus. It would simply be a scholastic achievement.

What I need to know are Bible promises. Short facts I can cling to without worrying about wording or knowing which chapter and verse they are in. I need to know there is no condemnation, even when I can't get out of bed.

If you find yourself where I've been far too often, I encourage you to remember that God doesn't cast us off just because we can't remember the details. He knows the shape of our memory. He knows the extent of our abilities and the extent of our pain.[xiii]

We can trust His love for us will never end, even when we don't know it's a promise found in Lamentations 3:22.

Live It

What are some Bible promises you can cling to when your pain is overwhelming? Add to my list above, and the list I started below.

- 1 Thessalonians 5:24
- Romans 8:1
- Lamentations 3:22
- _____
- _____
- _____

See It

These words that I command you today
shall be on your heart. You shall bind them as a
sign on your hand, and they shall be as frontlets
between your eyes. You shall write them on the
doorposts of your house and on your gates.
Deuteronomy 6:6, 8-9

When my twins were infants, I had a Scripture about Jesus calming the storm written on a note card and taped to the door of their room. It was during that season of life when I first started clinging to Jesus. I was learning how practical faith is.

I will never forget the night my family and I were coming

down a mountain in the middle of a blizzard. My husband looked calm and collected as he drove through the near white-out conditions. Our kids slept peacefully in the back seat, and I was nearing panic. At some point that year, I had written out Joshua 1:9 and taped it to the steering wheel of our van.

"Have I not commanded you? Be strong and courageous. Do not be afraid; do not be discouraged, for the Lord your God will be with you wherever you go." I couldn't read those words from the passenger seat, but I knew what they said. And I knew the answer to my rising fear was Jesus. I prayed the entire way down the mountain.

Those are just two examples of how I have clung to Scripture, but they are two of my founding experiences. Since then, I have learned one of the best ways to cling to Jesus, is to have small reminders of who He is all around me. Being able to see God's Word has a way of hiding it in your heart, even when you aren't being intentional.

As I have faced chronic migraines these past few years, I have found an even deeper appreciation for surrounding myself with Scripture. When you are in pain, especially when your head hurts, memorizing Scripture becomes exceedingly difficult.

On my desk, I have some Scripture stickers designed to point you to Jesus when you're anxious. Instead of using them as stickers though, I have them propped up like notecards. I have about five that I rotate through every so often: Romans 8:28, Luke 11:9, Exodus 14:14, Luke 18:27, Luke 22:42, and Romans 5:3. They remind me that no matter how bad the pain becomes, God is still good.

When my migraines first started, I had Psalm 118:17 written on my whiteboard. It says, "I shall not die, but I shall live, and recount the deeds of the Lord." I have spent a good deal of time writing out how God has blessed me, even when I am in pain.

Whether it's the wallpaper on your phone or a sticky note on your computer, having key Scriptures where you need them is a great reminder that you aren't alone. You can get knickknacks at Hobby Lobby or Christian bookstore with verses on them as well. But it doesn't have to be pretty or perfect. Every Bible verse you have where you can see it is an opportunity to read God's Word. Each verse is a reminder that you aren't alone, no matter how badly you hurt.

Live It

How can you surround yourself with Scripture? Which Bible verses speak to your hurt? If you are being intentional about surrounding yourself with Scripture, where can you place each verse?

- _____
- _____
- _____

Hear It

> So faith comes from hearing, and hearing through the word of Christ.
> Romans 10:17

Over the past several years, I've learned that if I don't stay tuned in to Jesus, it's not just my overall faith that suffers; it's virtually every aspect of it. If I don't spend time surrounding myself with God's Word, I pray less. My pain distracts me easier. I feel more alone in my struggle, even though I know deep down that Jesus is always with me.

When my head hurts and reading the Bible is virtually impossible, I've found listening to God's Word helps me connect with Jesus.

There were entire months I couldn't make it to church. Just taking a shower would cause my head to hurt so bad I had to go back to bed. Sitting through Sunday School and an hour-long worship service was simply impossible. Thankfully, when Covid-19 shutdown churches, many of them (including mine), began livestreaming. So even when I can't make it to church, I can still worship with my church family.

When my migraines first started, and reading my Bible became too hard, I started to use the Bible Gateway audio app to listen to the Word. I would choose a book of the Bible and just hit play.

Last year, a friend introduced me to the YouVersion app. I had heard of it before, but I never realized they had Bible reading plans you could listen to. This was a game changer for me. In 2020, I did a Chronological one-year reading plan with some other women, and I loved it. I've chosen a different one-year plan for 2021. I'm able to listen to it on my smartphone, and it keeps track of where I'm at.

Years ago, I bought my husband an audio Bible. It's on multiple CDs that he can play in his car on the way to work. If you don't have a smartphone, or good internet access, this can be a great alternative.

If you don't have the brainpower to dig into God's Word, listening to it can be a game changer. However, you can also listen to other resources that can help you grow your faith.

Before my head started hurting all the time, I was an avid reader. I would read multiple books every month. The migraines put an end to that, but I can still read thanks to audiobooks. I've also listened to some wonderful podcasts over the years. Anything to help me cling to Jesus, even if I'm lying there with my eyes closed.

Live It

Write down some ways you can listen to the Word of God. I've created an outline below to help you get started:

- **Audio Bible**
  - _____
  - _____

- **Sermons**
  - _____
  - _____
  - _____

- **Christian Audiobooks**
  - _____
  - _____
  - _____

- **Podcasts**
  - _____
  - _____
  - _____

Befriend It

> No longer do I call you servants, for the servant does not know what his master is doing; but I have called you friends, for all that I have heard from my Father I have made known to you.
> John 15:15

I chuckled when Bianca Olthoff called Paul her Bible Boyfriend, but I never forgot it. In fact, it encouraged me to make some Bible Besties of my own.

It's easy to read about the people in the Bible and put them on a shelf; as if they belong next to Mary Poppins, Winnie-the-Pooh, and Stuart Little. But they are in an entirely different category.

While the Weasley twins are a fantastic work of imagination, Shadrach, Meshach, and Abednego were real people. The stuff they went through actually happened. The thorn in Paul's flesh that God wouldn't take away was a real struggle for a real man, and I can totally relate to that.

Job was a man dedicated to serving God, and all of his children died. He went from living the high life to losing virtually everything. His life kept getting worse. First, he lost his earthly treasures, then he got sick, and then his friends came over and told him it was all his fault.

As a woman in the midst of a battle with chronic pain, Job has a special place in my heart. One month, I was hiking in the mountains of Colorado with the kids in our youth group, and the next I was bedridden. Life really does change just that fast.

Job reminds me that no matter how bad it hurts, there is hope. God restored Job's fortune. Even though his new children would never replace those he lost, and he would never get back the time he was sick, there was still a light at the end of the tunnel. I don't know if God will ever make me pain-free this side of Heaven, but even if He doesn't, I know this world isn't all there is. There will come a day when God will wipe away our tears and there will be no more pain.[xiv]

Peter walked on water. When his gaze shifted from Jesus to the waves, he started to sink. His story reminds me that when I start floundering, I need to refocus on Jesus.

And then there's Shadrach, Meshach, and Abednego. God didn't put out the flames in the fiery furnace. He didn't keep them from going in. He went in with them. They remind me I'm not in this alone.

These Bible Besties remind me who my God is, and that I'm not alone in my struggles. When I am having a bad day, they often come to mind as sweet spiritual friends reminding me to endure. To fight the good fight of faith.[xv]

Live It

Can you think of anyone from the Bible who could relate to your pain? Add some Bible Besties of your own to my list below.

- Shadrach, Meshach, and Abednego
- Job
- Peter
- Paul
- _____
- _____
- _____

Spill It

> Bear one another's burdens,
> and so fulfill the law of Christ.
> Galatians 6:2

Pain can feel very lonely. Especially if it keeps you from getting out and fellowshipping with other believers, or even family outings. Chronic pain can isolate you.

After being in pain for over a year, I was lonely and frustrated. I felt ostracized from everyone I knew. That's not to say I was alone, because I wasn't. I have a ton of prayer warriors. People from my church family, my Candid Gals, and others from around the world pray for me every day. I cherish their prayers; however, they are all praying for my migraines.

Over the past three plus years, I have faced some huge struggles that had nothing to do with my head hurting. They were all in addition to it, but often completely unrelated.

I remember going up to the altar for prayer one Sunday, and being surrounded by people who loved me. Yet not a single one of them asked why I needed prayer. They just assumed it was because my head hurt and prayed for that. As much as I appreciated the prayers, I have never felt as alone as I did in that moment surrounded by prayer warriors.

The hard truth was that I was facing a huge personal battle and really wanted to tell someone who could pray with me. I needed to spill my heart, but I didn't get the chance. Months later, I realized I let my chronic pain isolate me. I let each of those wonderful prayer warriors keep praying instead of speaking up and asking for someone to pray with me about what else was going on. It wasn't their fault I felt alone; it was my own.

Thankfully, in the time since then, I have found an incredible prayer partner. She touches base with me consistently to ask how I'm doing. Not if my head hurts, but me. She asks about my kids. She asks about work. She digs in and wants to know what I want prayer for. Because I'm in pain all the time, I often take her for granted. She usually has to send the first text message, but I can't imagine where I would be without her. She keeps me connected even though I never leave the house. She also helps me focus on more than my pain.

At one point, I had become bitter. My head hurt and when people would ask me to pray for them, I got frustrated. Like, obviously my prayers weren't working. However, I've discovered that praying for someone else does wonders for me spiritually. It shifts my focus away from the pain and reminds me that prayer does work. I don't know why God hasn't taken away my pain, but I have seen Him answer other prayers.

Live It

Who can you talk to about becoming a prayer and accountability partner? Make sure you let them know you need someone who can check in with you periodically and pray about more than your pain.

Play It

Oh come, let us worship and bow down; let us kneel before the Lord, our Maker!
Psalm 95:6

Praise and worship music holds a special place in my heart. Playing songs like "God is Always Good," helps me refocus no matter how bad my head hurts. Songs like "Blessings" by Laura Story remind me I'm not alone in my pain.

One Sunday at church, we were singing "Living Hope" when it hit me: Jesus died on the cross for me. He was beaten, flogged, whipped, and tortured. I can't imagine the pain He endured for us. Yet it was the first time I had been to church in months because of my chronic pain. The realization broke my heart.

Yet I also know He understands my pain and would still give His life for mine, even if I never made it to church again. That's how much He loves us. Our salvation isn't dependent on whether or not we push through the pain. It isn't dependent on anything we do. God is our "Good, Good Father,"[xvi] and we are loved by Him. Nothing will ever change that.

Even beyond the reminders we find in praise and worship songs, praising God is good for the soul. We were created to give God glory. Praising Him through the pain keeps my focus where it belongs—on Christ alone.

Instead of being consumed by the pain, singing along with worship music reminds me that life isn't all about me. It helps me cling to Jesus no matter how bad the pain is.

When I was first hospitalized in 2017, I remember tuning the TV in my room to the Christian music channel, and then hiding my eyes from the light. The lights in my room were always off, but the Christian music playing quietly in the background set the tone.

Even the nurses commented on what a joy it was to come into my room. I was in no state to witness to anyone, but they could all tell I was different. Not just because of the music, but because of the way I treated them and conducted myself through the pain.

I don't say any of this to my credit, all the glory goes to

God. I know without a shadow of a doubt that without Him in my life, I wouldn't be the person I am today. And I have no idea how I would face every day with a migraine without Him in my life. He is what keeps me going, and I can think of nothing better than to praise Him through the pain.

Live It

I have created a playlist full of worship songs I listen to that help me focus on Jesus when I'm in pain. You can find my *Worship Music for When You Struggle with Chronic Pain* playlist on YouTube by visiting: ChronicPainandJesus.com/youtube and on Spotify at: ChronicPainandJesus.com/spotify.

I would encourage you to consider making your own praise and worship playlist or bookmarking mine. Some of the songs on my list include:

- "God is Always Good" by Covenant Worship
- "Into the Sea" by Tasha Layton
- "Even If" by Mercy Me
- "On My Knees" by Jaci Velasquez
- "Need You Now" by Plumb
- "Blessings" by Laura Story
- "Way Maker" by Leeland
- "Living Hope" by Phil Wickham
- "Chain Breaker" by Zach Williams
- "Trust in You" by Lauren Daigle
- "Eye of the Storm" by Ryan Stevenson
- "He Will Hold Me Fast" by Keith & Kristyn

Getty
- "Battle Belongs" by Phil Wickham
- "Shoulders" by For King and Country
- "Through the Fire" by Hawk Nelson
- "Amen" by I am They
- "Storms" by V. Rose
- "Lord I Need You" by Chris Tomlin
- "You Raise Me Up" by Selah
- "You Carry Me" by Moriah Peters
- "Not for a Moment" by Meredith Andrews
- "Oceans" by Hillsong
- "Without You" by For Kind and Country
- "God on the Mountain" by Lynda Randle
- "O' Lord" by Lauren Daigle
- "No Matter What" by Kerrie Roberts
- "Steady" by For King and Country
- "I Am Not Alone" by Kari Jobe
- "Hills and Valleys" by Tauren Wells
- "I Know" by Big Daddy Weave
- "One Day at a Time" by Christy Lane

Which songs help you cling to Jesus when life is hard?

- _____
- _____
- _____

Embrace It

> I have said these things to you, that in me
> you may have peace. In the world you
> will have tribulation. But take heart;
> I have overcome the world.
> John 16:33

KLU GIB.

Keep Looking Up, God Is Bigger.

A sweet author friend of mine used that acronym to encourage me one day, and it really struck home. It's virtually the essence of our faith. No matter how bad the pain is, God is bigger.

My experience with chronic pain hasn't been easy, but I know I can face each day with Jesus. As I have been writing this book, our pastor has been preaching a sermon series through the Book of Ecclesiastes. Next to Ecclesiastes three in my Bible, I wrote the words: *A time for pain and a time to heal.* I am thrilled that a doctor seems to have found a medication that is effectively decreasing my pain. However, I know whether God is granting me a short reprieve or bringing me to the end of my chronic pain journey, He is always good.

My prayer is that this has encouraged you in your struggle with pain. And no matter what, I hope you cling to Jesus—the Author and Perfector of our faith. Don't let your pain consume you, but instead renew your mind in Christ each and every day. The pain might not go away, but we can find comfort in the fact that Jesus overcame the world.

I want to leave you with a few short reminders.

First, give yourself grace, but don't give up.

Life is hard, and life with chronic pain can seem unbearable. There are days you might not get out of bed, but God can meet you right where you lay. He will never give up on you. He won't look at you and shake His head because you let the pain get the best of you. He will simply love you, because God is love.

Next, we are saved by grace alone, by faith alone, in Christ alone.

Our salvation isn't up to us. There's a meme that goes around Facebook every so often about the Passover.

The Israelites were responsible for putting the blood on the door, but that's as far as the Spirit of the Lord went. He didn't go inside of each house to see who was there or if they were deserving. As long as there was blood, they were good. That is what the blood of Christ is for us. He did it all when He died on the cross. We don't even have to smear it on the doorposts. Which brings me to the last point…

There is no condemnation for those of us who belong to Jesus.

When Jesus died on the cross, He said, "It is finished."[xvii] He did it all. There is nothing left for us to do other than to rest in Him. We belong to Jesus, and nothing or no one can take that away from us.[xviii]

I don't know if God will heal us this side of Heaven, but I know there will come a day with no more pain.[xix] That's something I can embrace, no matter how bad the pain is.

Before You Go

You can download printable quotes, Scriptures, and lists for *Clinging to Jesus* by visiting:
ChronicPainandJesus.com/printables

About Heather Hart

Heather Hart is an internationally best-selling and award-winning author with an unquenchable passion for Jesus… and she has had her life turned upside-down by chronic pain. In the summer of 2017, Heather was hospitalized with meningitis. She went from doing seven-mile hikes to basically bed-ridden overnight. While the meningitis only lasted for three weeks, the migraine is still going strong. Chronic pain and Jesus—that's how Heather describes her days.

Heather and her husband live in a small Texas town with five fun-filled teens and four kooky cats. Let's just say she doesn't always get the quiet atmosphere her introverted personality and chronic migraines crave, but she loves them all like crazy and wouldn't trade it for the world.

Despite her pain, God has given Heather a heart for ministering to women of all ages; helping them grow in their walk with Him. Her goal isn't to teach women how they can do more, be better, or achieve perfection, it's to point them to Jesus. Her mantra is "life is hard, God is good, and the gospel is a balm for the soul."

You can read Heather's full story by visiting ChronicPainandJesus.com/history

Coming Soon

Have you ever felt overwhelmed by all the six-step prayer plans?

Felt guilty about not having a war room or committing an hour to prayer each day?

In *Talking with Jesus*, Heather Hart and Valerie Riese share their own stories about breaking free from common prayer life expectations.

In this book you will learn:

- How to Break Free of Prayer Life Idolatry
- Secrets to Developing a Prayer Strategy that Works for You
- Types of Prayer Strategies for When You Need A Somewhere To Start

Plus, Heather and Valerie share relatable insights from

real-life. They aren't going to tell you how to be better, do more, or achieve perfection. They are going to help you break free of expectations and pray in a way that works for you.

Ladies, it's time to reclaim our prayer life.

Recommended Resources

The Clinging Cross

The Clinging Cross is a small cross, crafted from olive wood pruned from the Holy Land in Israel. It fits in the palm of your hand, so you can literally cling to it. I purchased mine from The Keeping Company, but they can also be found on Amazon.

Scripture Stickers

Hope Fuel has "Scripture Stickers" that are specifically designed to give you hope from God's Word. Each sticker is five inches wide. They are white with gold foil lettering and absolutely beautiful in their simplicity.

A Gospel Primer for Christians

Milton Vincent says the gospel is a gift that keeps on giving us everything we need for life and godliness. His book, *A Gospel Primer for Christians,* contains a gospel narrative in both prose and poetic form. I highly recommend it for every Christian, but especially those in pain who want to speak the gospel to themselves daily.

Stress Relief Aromatherapy Lotion

When you are overwhelmed by pain, the smell of this lotion from Bath & Body Works helps you breathe a little deeper. It is my absolute favorite lotion.

You can find these resources and more here:
ChronicPainandJesus.com/resources

Notes

[i] Zelaya, Carla E., James M. Dahlhamer, Jacqueline W. Lucas, and Eric M. Connor. "Chronic Pain and High-Impact Chronic Pain Among U.S. Adults, 2019." CDC. Centers for Disease Control and Prevention, November 4, 2020. https://www.cdc.gov/nchs/products/databriefs/db390.htm.
[ii] Romans 12:2a
[iii] 2 Timothy 3:16-17
[iv] Psalm 17:6; 1 John 5:14
[v] Matthew 11:28-29
[vi] Matthew 28:20
[vii] Isaiah 53
[viii] Matthew 26:36-44
[ix] John 16:25
[x] Psalm 94:18-19
[xi] Holy Bible, New International Version®, NIV® Copyright ©1973, 1978, 1984, 2011 by Biblica, Inc.® Used by permission. All rights reserved worldwide.
[xii] Romans 8:1
[xiii] Psalm 139
[xiv] Revelation 21:4
[xv] 1 Timothy 6:12
[xvi] "Good, Good Father." Written by Tony Brown and Pat Barrett. Performed by Chris Tomlin
[xvii] John 19:30
[xviii] Romans 8:38-39
[xix] Revelation 21:4

Manufactured by Amazon.ca
Bolton, ON